Annual Survey of Jails in Indian Country, 2016–2019

Eligibility

Eligible applicants are national, regional, state, or local public and private entities, including for-profit and nonprofit organizations, faith-based and community organizations, institutions of higher education, federally recognized Indian tribal governments as determined by the Secretary of the Interior, and units of local government that support initiatives for improving the functioning of the criminal justice system.

Under section 302 of the Omnibus Crime Control and Safe Streets Act, BJS is authorized to make grants to, or enter into contracts or cooperative agreements with, states (including territories), units of local government, federally recognized American Indian and Alaska Native Tribal governments as determined by the Secretary of the Interior, nonprofit and for-profit organizations (including tribal nonprofit or for-profit organizations), institutions of higher education (including tribal institutions of higher education), and certain qualified individuals. For-profit organizations must agree to forgo any profit or management fee. Foreign governments, foreign organizations, and foreign institutions of higher education are not eligible to apply.

BJS welcomes applications that involve two or more entities, however, one eligible entity must be the applicant and the other(s) must be proposed as subrecipient(s). The applicant must be the entity with primary responsibility for conducting and leading the proposed project. If successful, the applicant will be responsible for monitoring and appropriately managing any subrecipients or, as applicable, for administering any procurement subcontracts that would receive federal program funds from the applicant under the award. Only one application per lead applicant will be considered; however, subrecipients may be part of multiple proposals.

BJS may elect to make awards for applications submitted under this solicitation in future fiscal years, dependent on the merit of the applications and on the availability of appropriations. For additional eligibility information, see Section C. Eligibility Information.

Deadline

Applicants must register with Grants.gov prior to submitting an application. All applications are due to be submitted and in receipt of a successful validation message in Grants.gov by 11:59 p.m. eastern time on May 26, 2015.

All applicants are encouraged to read this Important Notice: Applying for Grants in Grants.gov.

For additional information, see How to Apply in Section D. Application and Submission Information.

Contact Information

For technical assistance with submitting an application, contact the Grants.gov Customer Support Hotline at 800-518-4726 or 606-545-5035, or via email to support@grants.gov. The Grants.gov Support Hotline hours of operation are 24 hours a day, 7 days a week, except federal holidays.

Applicants that experience unforeseen Grants.gov technical issues beyond their control that prevent them from submitting their application by the deadline must e-mail the BJS contact identified below **within 24 hours after the application deadline** and request approval to submit their application. Additional information on reporting technical issues is found under "Experiencing Unforeseen Grants.gov Technical Issues" in the How to Apply section.

For assistance with any other requirements of this solicitation, contact Todd D. Minton, BJS Statistician, by telephone at 202-307-0765, or by email at askbjs@usdoj.gov. Include "SJIC" in the subject line.

Grants.gov number assigned to this announcement: BJS-2015-4166

Release date: March 24, 2015

Contents

Annual Survey of Jails in Indian Country, 2016–2019

(CFDA # 16.734)

A. Program Description

Overview

This award will provide funding through a cooperative agreement to administer annually the Survey of Jails in Indian Country (SJIC) data collection and analysis activities for four iterations of the survey: 2016, 2017, 2018, and 2019. The SJIC is used to describe changes in the inmate population of jails in Indian country and how these facilities are staffed and operated. Intermittently, via addenda, the SJIC also is used to collect data on the programs and services these facilities provide, such as those related to inmate health care, medical assessments, mental health screening procedures, counseling programs, and education programs.

Authorizing Legislation: Under section 302 of the Omnibus Crime Control and Safe Streets Act, BJS is authorized to "make grants to, or enter into cooperative agreements or contracts with public agencies, institutions of higher education, private organizations, or private individuals" to collect and analyze criminal justice statistics. BJS is also authorized to "collect and analyze statistical information, concerning the operations of the criminal justice system at the Federal, State, tribal, and local levels."

Program-Specific Information

The SJIC collects information from all known *operating* confinement facilities, detention centers, and other correctional facilities (80 as of 2014) operated by tribal authorities or the Bureau of Indian Affairs (BIA). The SJIC collects information pertaining to jail inmate population counts, movements, and characteristics on the last weekday in the month of June each year. Data are collected on the number of adults and juveniles held, gender of inmates, conviction status, seriousness of inmates' offenses, number of admissions and releases during the month of June, number of inmate deaths, average daily population, peak population during the month of June, rated capacity of facility, crowding issues, and jail staffing and training. Intermittently BJS also collects data, via an addendum to the core survey, on the physical conditions and operations of Indian country facilities. The addendum requests information on inmate medical services, mental health services, suicide prevention procedures, substance dependency programs, domestic violence counseling, sex offender treatment, educational programs, and inmate work assignments.

Copies of data collection instruments used for the 2013 SJIC and the last survey addendum, conducted in 2011, can be found at www.bjs.gov/index.cfm?ty=dcdetail&iid=276.

Data from the SJIC collection are published in an annual *Jails in Indian Country* series of bulletins, available at www.bjs.gov/index.cfm?ty=pbse&sid=32.

Goals, Objectives, Deliverables, and Expected Scholarly Products

The goals of this project are to field the survey instrument and to analyze the data it collects to produce high quality and accurate data and analyses for the 2016 through 2019 iterations of the SJIC. In addition, BJS expects the award recipient to recommend enhancements for the Survey. Annual data collection and analytic activities include the following:

- fielding the survey
- following up, as necessary, to obtain the high response rates that have been a hallmark of this collection (e.g., 100% in 2008–12; 90% or greater in 2013 or prior years)
- implementing data entry, verification, and editing procedures to complete an analytic dataset that will be used to prepare tables for release in BJS's annual bulletins on Jails in Indian Country
- delivering the analytic dataset to BJS in a timely manner to allow for BJS analysis for the annual bulletins
- preparing tables for the BJS annual bulletins
- delivering a final dataset and documentation that will be used for archiving the data at the National Archive of Criminal Justice Data (NACJD), available at www.icpsr.umich.edu/NACJD/index.html.

The award recipient must meet the critical objectives each year of the SJIC, from 2016 through 2019, as shown in Table 1. In addition to the annual objectives, two one-time objectives must be met: (1) fielding an addendum to the 2019 version of the SJIC, and (2) recommending enhancements for the SJIC. Pending funding and budget and other clearances, the project will begin on March 1, 2016, and terminate on June 30, 2020.

As befitting a cooperative agreement, BJS will work collaboratively with the data collection agent to address issues and concerns that arise during survey administration and analysis, as well as improvements to the survey. BJS maintains all final decision making authority regarding the implementation of the SJIC collection. Survey instrument design and publication and dissemination of the final product are the sole responsibilities of BJS.

BJS retains all rights to exclusive use of the data until it releases the public-use dataset, which will be available to the public via the Internet and at the National Criminal Justice Data Archives at the University of Michigan. The recipient shall not release or disclose any data collected through this cooperative agreement without prior written approval from BJS or until the dataset has been released to the public. This includes, but is not limited to, presentations at professional conferences and meetings, press releases, and grant applications. Unauthorized release of the data by the recipient or its associates may result in the immediate commencement of termination or suspension proceedings in accordance with 28 CFR Part 18.

The data collection agent is expected to have routine contact with tribal authorities and Bureau of Indian Affairs (BIA) law enforcement and correctional agencies and must be knowledgeable about tribal law enforcement and corrections. The award recipient should also be knowledgeable regarding survey nonresponse bias analysis and variance estimation.

Annual Tasks

Applicants' proposals should describe their plan for addressing the following 12 annual tasks. In describing their plans, applicants should clearly define the relationship between the annual tasks and the annual project objectives.

1. Submit to BJS a detailed timetable for each project year. Meet with BJS within 2 weeks of the start of the project and at the beginning of each subsequent project year to discuss the project's scope of work and draft timetable. Revise the draft as necessary based on BJS comments. After the BJS project manager agrees to the timetable, the recipient should work toward achieving each task by its scheduled date.

2. Update and maintain an accurate contact list of the SJIC respondents. Using BJS's most recent list of SJIC respondents and Indian country jail facilities, verify and update the names, addresses, and appropriate contact information of each respondent. Search for additional jail facilities operated by tribal authorities or BIA that are not included on the BJS list using the information sources available to the award recipient (including any experience the recipient may have had with specific BIA and tribal law enforcement and correctional agencies, commercial databases, membership lists of professional associations, academic researchers specializing in jail research, and other sources). Review newly identified jail facilities with BJS to determine whether to include them in the survey, and add to the list those respondents that BJS and the recipient decide fall within the scope of the SJIC collection.

    For planning purposes, assume that there are 80 respondents (the number in the 2014 active survey administration). BJS will provide a final list of the operating facilities prior to survey implementation. The BJS bulletin, *Jails in Indian Country, 2013,* lists the 2013 facilities in the appendix tables available at: www.bjs.gov/index.cfm?ty=pbse&sid=32. There are a small number of facilities each year that are nonoperational, but are considered to be within the scope of the SJIC and are assessed annually.

3. Field the SJIC. Use the current version of the SJIC instrument that has been approved by OMB, available at www.bjs.gov/index.cfm?ty=dcdetail&iid=276.

    Fielding the SJIC involves sending notification letters 2 weeks prior to faxing or mailing the survey (assume fax administration for planning purposes) and a cover letter from BJS that describes the survey, indicates the target dates for completion, and names contact persons on the award recipient's staff and from BJS staff. C ommunicate with respondents about the upcoming survey using the method they prefer (e.g., fax, mail, or email).

    The award recipient will prepare drafts of the notification and cover letters and submit them to BJS for review. After BJS's approval, the award recipient will distribute the notification letters and cover letters with the survey questionnaire. Historically, the SJIC has been administered as a paper form, primarily by fax. While following up with respondents, the award recipient should determine the most favorable mode for administering the survey and determine the feasibility of administering the SJIC using an electronic collection method. In this assessment, the award recipient should consider cost-effective approaches, tribal access to electronic reporting, reducing respondent burden, and reducing the time needed to complete the data collection while maintaining high

6
BJS-2015-4166

quality data. The recipient should assess the information it obtains about respondents' capacities to provide data electronically and include this assessment in the one-time task of recommending enhancements to the SJIC.

4. Follow up as needed with respondents that require assistance, clarification, or encouragement to complete the survey during the data collection period. This may involve multiple follow-up telephone calls, re-mailing or re-faxing surveys, and phone, fax, or email correspondence. BJS has found faxing to be effective in administering the survey and conducting follow-up.

   During follow up, if information is obtained that is suggestive of new facilities in Indian country that are not included in the respondent list, verify the existence of each facility and obtain contact information for it. Identify facilities that closed, merged with another facility, or whose operations were suspended during a year. Update the respondent list with information about new or closed facilities.

5. Identify and implement techniques needed to achieve a 95% or better survey and item response rate as specified in the "Performance Measures" section on page 18. BJS has consistently achieved greater than a 95% response rate and obtained a 100% response rate during the 2008–12 survey administration. If necessary, the recipient will conduct a historical review of respondent data from previous JIC survey administrations to validate current responses.

6. Implement and maintain a database to provide ongoing, real-time status of the progress of the survey administration. Use the database to provide project status information about each respondent, including a record of follow-up communication and procedures used for each case, the respondent's method of response (i.e., mail, email, fax, or phone), and dates of contacts and survey completion. The database should remain current, and requests for information should be accessible to the BJS project manager at all times.

7. Maintain and update a database of survey responses as surveys are received, with the goal of completing the review, assessment, data entry, and edit check for each survey within 2 weeks of receipt. Within that time frame, address survey response issues, such as clarifying discrepancies in responses, correcting errors in entry, and addressing item nonresponse.

8. Prepare data tables for inclusion in the BJS bulletin series *Jails in Indian Country* as specified by BJS. For all years, produce four facility-level tables to be included in the midyear report. These tables will include information on inmate custody counts and crowding, the number of adults and juveniles held in Indian country jails, and the type of offense and conviction status for the confined inmate population. For planning purposes, see table 8 and the appendix tables included in the *Jails in Indian Country, 2013* report. Tables should be generated directly from the database using software that can meet BJS formatting requirements (such as Excel, .csv files, and .pdf files).

9. Submit data to BJS for archiving. Submit a final electronic version of the survey data with any BJS modifications and additions, such as BJS's calculated variables, for archiving. BJS will deliver to the award recipient a copy of the final version of the data that it used to produce the annual bulletin on *Jails in Indian Country*, and this version of the dataset is

the one to be archived. In addition, organize and develop the appropriate documentation for archiving the Jails in Indian Country data at the National Archive of Criminal Justice Data (NACJD) at the University of Michigan, available at www.icpsr.umich.edu/NACJD/index.html. The data and documentation for archiving are to be submitted to BJS for review and modified if needed based on BJS comments. BJS will transmit the data and documentation to NACJD.

Data and documentation to be provided for archiving include—

- An electronic copy of the data for each reference year (that is, the year to which the data pertain), including any modifications to data originally submitted to BJS and any BJS-created variables.

- Copies of the programming code, for reproducing all constructed measures and original data analysis, and other programming code from database queries, images, or PowerPoint slides. BJS will give the grantee copies of computer code that it uses to generate created variables. The recipient will compile this into the set of documentation to be submitted for archiving.

- A codebook listing the data variables, variable labels, value labels, and missing value designations.

- A blank electronic version of each data collection instrument.

- Manual, electronic, or other data collection protocols.

- Blank consent forms, as applicable.

- A copy of the annual bulletin associated with a reference year of data.

Based on the NACJD staff's review of the materials submitted for archiving the SJIC data, the recipient may need to provide additional data or documentation. No release or use of the data (including presentations and publications) can take place prior to the release of the public use dataset without written permission from the BJS Director.

10. Respond, from time-to-time, to requests for special tabulations of the SJIC data. These involve producing descriptive statistics, trends over time for selected facilities, and other fairly rudimentary analyses that should require no more than 1 day of an analyst's time. The recipient will produce and verify the program code used to generate the tabulations and submit it to BJS. For planning purposes, the award recipient should expect to conduct three such analyses.

11. Attend a major conference or meeting of Indian country officials to present on issues related to the Jails in Indian Country project. The conference presentation tasks may include (a) leading focus groups to obtain feedback about the survey for the purposes of enhancing the survey, or (b) presenting at BIA manager meetings about the SJIC. Possible venues include the National Indian Nations Conference and the American Jail Association's annual conference. Based on recommendations from the award recipient, the BJS project manager will make the final decisions about conference venues.

12. Maintain regular communication with BJS staff about the project's status, including regular phone calls, meetings as necessary, and monthly project status reports. The monthly status reports shall be submitted by the middle of each month and shall describe

the status of the project relative to its goals (such as collection year comparison of response rates by weeks in the field, response rates, item nonresponse, information about new or closed facilities, changes in facility operations, and other factors related to the scope of coverage), implementation issues needing special attention, problems encountered needing BJS input, objectives for the upcoming month, and a comparison of response rates of the current survey to those of previous surveys based on time in the field. These should be provided to BJS via email in commercially available software beginning 1 month after the survey fielding date as identified on the questionnaire.

The final monthly report for a survey year will include a review of the survey's performance for that year. Items to include in this report are final response and item rates, collection issues and concerns, extent of respondent burden, and other survey administration issues that imposed a relatively large burden on the respondents or the award recipient in administering the survey.

One-Time Tasks

The following two tasks will be completed during the 4-year project period.

1. Field an addendum to the SJIC during the 2019 data collection. The addendum will focus on topics that were addressed in the 2011 survey addendum, which can be found at www.bjs.gov/index.cfm?ty=dcdetail&iid=276. In addition to the four tables produced annually, in the 2019 data collection year, produce approximately 12 facility-level tables on programs and services based on the results from the survey addendum. See *Jails in Indian Country, 2011* for an example of the facility-level tables produced from the addendum, available at www.bjs.gov/index.cfm?ty=pbdetail&iid=1009.

2. Make recommendations to BJS for enhancing the SJIC. Throughout the SJIC, the recipient should use the annual tasks to identify opportunities to enhance the SJIC and obtain and assess the information necessary to make informed recommendations for these enhancements. Specifically, during the start of the second project year, the award recipient should propose to BJS a concept paper for undertaking this assessment of opportunity, and if additional tasks are required to complete it, provide BJS with an estimate of the costs to complete them. The recipient should review the data collection instrument, identify gaps in the collection, assess the costs and challenges associated with obtaining data to fill gaps, and develop methodologies for obtaining the data. This process should involve key stakeholders. The review and assessment should cover all aspects of the SJIC, including the content of the survey, modes of administration, communication with the field about the survey, statistical products from the data collection, and dissemination of products.

At the end of the review, submit to BJS a document that summarizes what was learned from the review and propose changes to the SJIC. This document should identify and describe potential improvements that could be made to the survey, its administration, or analysis that can be implemented during future iterations of the survey. Include recommendations to BJS that will lead to improved response rates, higher quality data, and a reduction in the time required for data collection.

Table 1. Key deliverables and deliverable dates for SJIC	
Key annual tasks and objectives	**Annual deliverable date**
Timetable, task plan, staff allocation	April 15
Complete data collection to BJS (including addendum in 2019)	December 15
Provide BJS with an analysis dataset	January 15
Provide BJS with statistical tables	February 1
Provide BJS with data and documentation for archiving the SJIC data	March 1
Final monthly report with annual review of survey performance	March 15
Other key tasks and objectives	
Submit concept paper to BJS for the SJIC assessment (one-time task #2)	July 15, 2017
Field addendum to the 2019 SJIC (one-time task #1)	June 20, 2019
Provide BJS with addendum-related statistical tables (one-time task #1)	February 1, 2020

In addition to required data sets, a draft and final summary overview of research results, interim and final progress and financial reports[1], BJS expects scholarly products to result from each award under this solicitation, taking the form of one or more published, peer-reviewed, scientific journal articles, and/or (if appropriate) law review journal articles, book chapter(s) or book(s) in the academic press, technological prototypes, patented inventions, or similar scientific products.

B. Federal Award Information

BJS expects to make one award for an estimated total of $400,000 for a 54-month project period beginning on January 4, 2016.

To allow time for, among other things, any necessary post-award review, modification, and clearance by OJP of the proposed budget, applicants should propose an award start date of January 4, 2016.

If the applicant is proposing a project that reasonably could be conducted in discrete phases, with each phase resulting in completion of one or more significant, defined milestones, then BJS strongly recommends that the applicant structure the application—specifically including the narrative, expected scholarly products, timelines/milestones, and budget detail worksheet and budget narrative—to clearly set out each phase. (This is particularly the case if the applicant proposes a project that will exceed—in cost or length of project period—the amount or length

---

[1] See "Federal Award Administration Information" ("General Information About Post-Federal Award Reporting Requirements") section of this solicitation, below, for additional information.

anticipated for an individual award (or awards) under this solicitation.) Given limitations on the availability to BJS of funds for its statistical mission, this information will assist BJS in considering whether partial funding of applications that would not receive full funding would be productive. (If BJS elects to fund only certain phases of a proposed project in FY 2015, the expected scholarly products from the partial-funding award may, in some cases, vary from those described above.)

All awards are subject to the availability of appropriated funds and to any modifications or additional requirements that may be imposed by law.

Type of Award[2]

BJS expects that it will make any award from this solicitation in the form of a cooperative agreement, which is a particular type of grant used because BJS expects to have ongoing substantial involvement in award activities. Substantial involvement includes direct oversight and involvement with the grantee organization in implementation of the grant, but does not involve day-to-day project management. See Administrative, National Policy, and other Legal Requirements, under Section F. Federal Award Administration, for details regarding the federal involvement anticipated under an award from this solicitation. As discussed later in the solicitation, important rules (including limitations) apply to any conference/meeting/training costs under cooperative agreements.

Please note: Any recipient of an award under this solicitation will be required to comply with Department of Justice regulations on confidentiality and human subjects' protection. See "Evidence, Research, and Evaluation Guidance and Requirements" under "Solicitation Requirements" in the OJP Funding Resource Center.

Financial Management and System of Internal Controls

If selected for funding, the award recipient must:

(a) Establish and maintain effective internal control over the federal award that provides reasonable assurance that the non-federal entity is managing the federal award in compliance with federal statutes, regulations, and the terms and conditions of the federal award. These internal controls should be in compliance with guidance in "Standards for Internal Control in the Federal Government" issued by the Comptroller General of the United States and the "Internal Control Integrated Framework," issued by the Committee of Sponsoring Organizations of the Treadway Commission (COSO).

(b) Comply with federal statutes, regulations, and the terms and conditions of the federal awards.

(c) Evaluate and monitor the non-federal entity's compliance with statute, regulations, and the terms and conditions of federal awards.

---

[2] *See generally* 31 U.S.C. §§ 6301–6305 (defines and describes various forms of federal assistance relationships, including grants and cooperative agreements (a type of grant)).

(d) Take prompt action when instances of noncompliance are identified including noncompliance identified in audit findings.

(e) Take reasonable measures to safeguard protected personally identifiable information and other information the federal awarding agency or pass-through entity designates as sensitive or the non-federal entity considers sensitive consistent with applicable federal, state, and local laws regarding privacy and obligations of confidentiality.

In order to better understand administrative requirements and cost principles, award applicants are encouraged to enroll, at no charge, in the Department of Justice Grants Financial Management Online Training available here.

Budget Information

What will not be funded:

- Proposals primarily to purchase equipment, materials, or supplies. (A budget may include these items if they are necessary to conduct data collection, research, development, demonstration, evaluation, or analysis.)

- Proposals that are not responsive to this specific solicitation.

Cost Sharing or Match Requirement

This solicitation does not require a match. However, if a successful application proposes a voluntary match amount, and OJP approves the budget, the total match amount incorporated into the approved budget becomes mandatory and subject to audit.

Pre-Agreement Cost Approvals

OJP does not typically approve pre-agreement costs; an applicant must request and obtain the prior written approval of OJP for all such costs. If approved, pre-agreement costs could be paid from grant funds consistent with a grantee's approved budget, and under applicable cost standards. However, all such costs prior to award and prior to approval of the costs are incurred at the sole risk of an applicant. Generally, no applicant should incur project costs *before* submitting an application requesting federal funding for those costs. Should there be extenuating circumstances that appear to be appropriate for OJP's consideration as pre-agreement costs, the applicant should contact the point of contact listed on the title page of this announcement for details on the requirements for submitting a written request for approval. See the section on Costs Requiring Prior Approval in the Financial Guide, for more information.

Limitation on Use of Award Funds for Employee Compensation; Waiver

With respect to any award of more than $250,000 made under this solicitation, recipients may not use federal funds to pay total cash compensation (salary plus cash bonuses) to any employee of the award recipient at a rate that exceeds 110% of the maximum annual salary payable to a member of the Federal Government's Senior Executive Service (SES) at an agency with a Certified SES Performance Appraisal System for that year.[3] The 2015 salary table for SES employees is available at the Office of Personnel Management website. Note: A recipient may compensate an employee at a greater rate, provided the amount in excess of this

---

[3] This limitation on use of award funds does not apply to the nonprofit organizations specifically named at appendix VIII to 2 CFR Part 200.

compensation limitation is paid with non-federal funds. (Any such additional compensation will not be considered matching funds where match requirements apply.)

Director of BJS may exercise discretion to waive, on an individual basis, the limitation on compensation rates allowable under an award. An applicant requesting a waiver should include a detailed justification in the budget narrative of the application. Unless the applicant submits a waiver request and justification with the application, the applicant should anticipate that OJP will request the applicant to adjust and resubmit the budget.

The justification should include the particular qualifications and expertise of the individual, the uniqueness of the service the individual will provide, the individual's specific knowledge of the program or project being undertaken with award funds, and a statement explaining that the individual's salary is commensurate with the regular and customary rate for an individual with his/her qualifications and expertise, and for the work to be done.

Prior Approval, Planning, and Reporting of Conference/Meeting/Training Costs
OJP strongly encourages applicants that propose to use award funds for any conference-, meeting-, or training-related activity to review carefully—before submitting an application—the OJP policy and guidance on "conference" approval, planning, and reporting available at www.ojp.gov/funding/confcost.htm. OJP policy and guidance (1) encourage minimization of conference, meeting, and training costs; (2) require prior written approval (which may affect project timelines) of most such costs for cooperative agreement recipients and of some such costs for grant recipients; and (3) set cost limits, including a general prohibition of all food and beverage costs.

Costs Associated with Language Assistance (if applicable)
If an applicant proposes a program or activity that would deliver services or benefits to individuals, the costs of taking reasonable steps to provide meaningful access to those services or benefits for individuals with limited English proficiency may be allowable. Reasonable steps to provide meaningful access to services or benefits may include interpretation or translation services where appropriate.

For additional information, see the "Civil Rights Compliance" section under "Solicitation Requirements" in the OJP Funding Resource Center.

C. Eligibility Information

Eligibility
For additional eligibility information, see Title page.

Cost Sharing or Match Requirement
For additional information on cost sharing and match requirement, see Section B. Federal Award Information.

Limit on Number of Application Submissions
If an applicant submits multiple versions of the same application, BJS will review only the most recent system-validated version submitted. For more information on system-validated versions, see How to Apply.

D. Application and Submission Information

What an Application Should Include
Applicants should anticipate that if they fail to submit an application that contains all of the specified elements, it may affect negatively the review of their application; and, should a decision be made to make an award, it may result in the inclusion of special conditions that preclude the recipient from accessing or using award funds pending satisfaction of the conditions.

Moreover, applicants should anticipate that applications determined to be nonresponsive to the scope of the solicitation, or that do not include the application elements that BJS has designated to be critical, will neither proceed to peer review nor receive further consideration. Under this solicitation, BJS has designated the following application elements as critical: Program Narrative, Budget Detail Worksheet, Budget Narrative, and resumes/curriculum vitae of key personnel. For purposes of this solicitation, "key personnel" means the principal investigator, and any and all co-principal investigators. Please review the "Note on File Names and File Types" under How to Apply to be sure applications are submitted in permitted formats.

OJP strongly recommends that applicants use appropriately descriptive file names (e.g., "Program Narrative," "Budget Detail Worksheet and Budget Narrative," "Timelines," "Memoranda of Understanding," "Resumes") for all attachments. Also, OJP recommends that applicants include resumes in a single file.

1. **Information to Complete the Application for Federal Assistance (SF-424)**
   The SF-424 is a required standard form used as a cover sheet for submission of pre-applications, applications, and related information. Grants.gov and OJP's Grants Management System (GMS) take information from the applicant's profile to populate the fields on this form. When selecting "type of applicant," if the applicant is a for-profit entity, select "For-Profit Organization" or "Small Business" (as applicable).

   Intergovernmental Review: This funding opportunity (program) **is not** subject to Executive Order 12372. (In completing the SF-424, applicants are to make the appropriate selection in response to question 19 to indicate that the "Program is not covered by E.O. 12372.")

2. **Project Abstract**
   The project abstract is a very important part of the application, and serves as an introduction to the proposed project. BJS uses the project abstract for a number of purposes, including the possible assignment of the application to a review panel. If the application is funded, the project abstract typically will become public information and be used to describe the project.

   Applications should include a high-quality project abstract that summarizes the proposed project in 250–400 words. Project abstracts should be—

   - Written for a general public audience.

   - Submitted as a separate attachment with "Project Abstract" as part of its file name.

   - Single-spaced, using a standard 12-point font (Times New Roman) with 1-inch margins.

As a separate attachment, the project abstract will **not** count against the page limit for the program narrative.

All project abstracts should follow the detailed template available at ojp.gov/funding/Apply/Resources/ProjectAbstractTemplate.pdf.

Permission to Share Project Abstract with the Public: It is unlikely that BJS will be able to fund all promising applications submitted under this solicitation, but it may have the opportunity to share information with the public regarding promising but unfunded applications, for example, through a listing on a webpage available to the public. The intent of this public posting would be to allow other possible funders to become aware of such proposals.

In the project abstract template, applicants are asked to indicate whether they give OJP permission to share their project abstract (including contact information) with the public if BJS does not fund the proposed project. Granting (or failing to grant) this permission will not affect OJP's funding decisions, and, if the application is not funded, granting permission will not guarantee that project abstract information will be shared, nor will it guarantee funding from any other source.

Note: OJP may choose not to list a project that otherwise would have been included in a listing of promising but unfunded applications, should the abstract fail to meet the format and content requirements noted above and outlined in the project abstract template.

3. **Program Narrative**

   The program narrative section of the application should not exceed 40 double-spaced pages in a 12-point font with 1-inch margins. If included in the main body of the program narrative, tables, charts, figures, and other illustrations count toward the 40-page limit for the narrative section. The project abstract, table of contents, appendices, and government forms do not count toward the 40-page limit.

   If the program narrative fails to comply with these length-related restrictions, BJS may consider such noncompliance in peer review and in final award decisions.

   The following sections should be included as part of the program narrative.[4]

   Program Narrative Guidelines:

   a. **Title Page** (not counted against the 40-page program narrative limit).

      The title page should include the title of the project, submission date, funding opportunity number, and the name and complete contact information (that is,

---

[4] As noted earlier, if the proposed program or project reasonably could be conducted in discrete phases, with each phase resulting in completion of one or more significant, defined milestones, then BJS strongly recommends that the applicant structure the application—specifically including the narrative, expected scholarly products, timelines/milestones, and budget detail worksheet and budget narrative—to set out each phase clearly. (In appropriate cases, the expected scholarly product(s) from a particular phase may vary from those described above.) See generally, "Goals, Objectives, Deliverables, and Expected Scholarly Products" under "Program-Specific Information," above.

address, telephone number, and e-mail address) for both the applicant organization and the principal investigator.

b. **Resubmit Response** (if applicable) (not counted against the 40-page program narrative limit).

If an applicant is resubmitting a proposal presented previously to BJS, but not funded, the applicant should indicate this. A statement should be provided, no more than two pages, addressing: (1) the title, submission date, and BJS-assigned application number of the previous proposal, and (2) a brief summary of revisions to the proposal, including responses to previous feedback received from BJS.

c. **Table of Contents and Figures** (not counted against the 40-page program narrative limit).

d. **Main Body.**

The main body of the program narrative should describe activities in the Statement of Work and address the evaluation criteria in depth. The narrative should also provide a detailed timeline and budget for project activities and demonstrate the applicant's capabilities for handling a national collection of criminal justice data. The following sections should be included as part of the program narrative:

- Statement of the Problem.

- Project Design and Implementation.

- Potential Impact.

- Capabilities/Competencies.

Within these sections, the narrative should address—

- Purpose, goals, and objectives.

- Review of relevant literature.

- Detailed description of research design and methods, such as research questions, hypotheses, description of sample, and analysis plan.

- Planned Scholarly Products (See Goals, Objectives, Deliverables, and Expected Scholarly Products under Program-Specific Information, above, for a discussion of expected scholarly products.

- Implications for criminal justice policy and practice in the United States.

- Management plan and organization.

- Data management plan

  All BJS-funded research requires development of a data management plan that guides data management activities throughout the agreement and ensures the timely release of the project's data and derived products after project completion. Applications must include a preliminary (2-page limit) data management plan that explains how data products will be developed, documented, formatted, and delivered to BJS in a manner that ensures optimal utility. Following funding of a proposal, the applicant will coordinate with an identified BJS data steward to develop a comprehensive data management plan which will be periodically reviewed and enhanced as the project evolves. The data management plan for this project is expected to address, at a minimum, the following:

  - Roles, rights, and responsibilities of all project participants
  - Expected data and metadata
  - Data formats, organization, and dissemination approach
  - Data retention and release timelines
  - Data security, confidentiality protection, and other policy requirements
  - Data archiving and preservation of access.

  At project completion, all data and complete metadata descriptions must be provided to the BJS data steward. In addition, BJS requires award recipients under this solicitation to submit to the National Archive of Criminal Justice Data (NACJD) at the University of Michigan (through BJS), all datasets that result in whole or in part from the work funded by BJS. These submissions must include all associated files and any documentation necessary to allow for future efforts by others to reproduce the project's findings and to extend the scientific value of the data set through such secondary analysis. All datasets and necessary documentation are to be submitted 90 days prior to the end of the project period. For more information, see the "Program Narrative" section of "What an Application Must Include." For information that BJS has previously agreed not to make publicly available for a period of time or that is undergoing review, data will be placed in a secure area until the period of exclusivity or review has expired.

- Plan for Dissemination to Broader Audiences (if applicable to the proposed project). Applicants should identify plans (if any) to produce or to make available to broader interested audiences—such as criminal/juvenile justice practitioners or policymakers—summary information from the planned scholarly products of the proposed project (such as summaries of articles in peer-reviewed scientific journals), in a form designed to be readily accessible and useful to those audiences. (Such dissemination might include, for example, trade press articles and webinars.)

e. Performance Measures

To assist the Department with fulfilling its responsibilities under the Government Performance and Results Act of 1993 (GPRA), Public Law 103-62, and the GPRA Modernization Act of 2010, Public Law 111-352, applicants that receive funding under this solicitation must provide data that measure the results of their work done under this solicitation. OJP will require any award recipient, post award, to provide the data requested in the "Data Grantee Provides" column so that OJP can calculate values for the "Performance Measures" column. (Submission of performance measures data is not required for the application.) Performance measures for this solicitation are as follows:

Objective	Performance Measure(s)	Data Grantee Provides	Description
Administer the Survey of Jails in Indian Country, and collect timely, complete, and accurate information on inmate counts and movements, facility operations and staff, inmate health care, and facility programs.	Achieve a 95% survey response rate	Number of agencies participating in the survey Number of agencies that responded to the surveys.	A response rate lower than 95% threshold is unacceptable. The minimum targets for missing or inconsistent files are: 1% on inmate counts and movements; inmate health care; and facility programs 5% maximum on facility staff.
	Percent of records in the database that are complete and accurate.	Complete and accurate data on jail inmate population counts, movements, and characteristics, including criteria outlined in the program-specific information section.	
	Number of scheduled data collection series and special analysis to be conducted.	Completion of the annual SJIC. Completion of the addendum to the SJIC.	
	Number of completed data collection on time.		

Provide statistical support to BJS to strengthen research and data collection activities, including enhancing SJIC.	Percentage of deliverables (including final reports and data files) that are completed on time. Percentage of deliverable (including final).	All applicable deliverables, as outlined in Table 1, including final reports and grantee statistical documents authored/co-authored with BJS.	Time from initiation of the collection to close of the reference period (target: 6 months for each reference year).
Disseminate SJIC data to external researchers.	Number of presentations conducted.	Number of presentations at professional or academic conferences.	

f. **Appendices** (not counted against the program narrative page limitation) include:

- Bibliography/references.

- Any tools/instruments, questionnaires, tables/charts/graphs, or maps pertaining to the proposed project that are supplemental to such items included in the main body of the narrative.

- Curriculum vitae or resumes of the principal investigator and any and all co-principal investigators. In addition, curriculum vitae, resumes, or biographical sketches of all other individuals (regardless of "investigator" status) who will be significantly involved in substantive aspects of the proposal (including, for example, individuals such as statisticians serving as consultants to conduct proposed data analysis).

  List (to the extent known) of all proposed project staff members, including those affiliated with the applicant organization or any proposed subrecipient organization(s), any proposed consultant(s) and contractors (whether individuals or organizations), and any proposed members of an advisory board for the project (if applicable). The list should include, for each individual and organization: name, title (if applicable), employer or other organizational affiliation, and roles and responsibilities proposed for the project.

- Proposed project timeline and expected milestones.

- A privacy certificate and human subjects protection certification of compliance must be completed for each project proposed in an application.

  - **Privacy Certification.** The privacy certificate is a funding recipient's certification of compliance with federal regulations requiring confidentiality of information identifiable to a private person, which is collected, analyzed, or otherwise used in connection with an OJP-funded research or statistical activity. The funding recipient's Privacy Certificate includes a description of its policies and procedures to be followed to protect identifiable data. A model certificate is located at www.bjs.gov/content/pub/pdf/bjsmpc.pdf.

  - **Human Subjects Protection Certification of Compliance.** BJS requires the funding recipient to submit proper documentation to be used to determine that the research project meets the federal requirements for human subjects protections set forth in 28 CFR Part 46. A model certificate, describing the necessary information to be provided by the funding recipient, can be accessed at www.bjs.gov/content/hscr.cfm.

- List of any previous and current BJS awards to applicant organization and investigator(s), including the BJS-assigned award numbers and a brief description of any scholarly products that resulted in whole or in part from work funded under the BJS award(s). (See "Goals, Objectives, Deliverables, and Expected Scholarly Products" under "Program-Specific Information," above, for definition of "scholarly products.")

- Letters of cooperation/support or administrative agreements from organizations collaborating in the project, such as law enforcement and correctional agencies (if applicable).

- List of other agencies, organizations, or funding sources to which this proposal has been submitted (if applicable).

- Data archiving plan. Applicants should anticipate that BJS will require (through special award conditions, including a partial withholding of award funds) that data sets resulting in whole or in part from projects funded under this solicitation be submitted to BJS for archiving with the National Archive of Criminal Justice Data (NACJD).

  Applications should include as an appendix a brief plan—labeled "Data Archiving Plan"—to comply with data archiving requirements. The plan should provide brief details about proposed data management and archiving, including submission to BJS (for NACJD) of **all files and documentation** necessary to allow for future efforts by others to reproduce the project's findings and/or to extend the scientific value of the data set through secondary analysis. Pertinent files and documentation include, among other things, qualitative and quantitative data produced, instrumentation and data collection forms, codebook(s), any specialized programming code necessary to reproduce all constructed measures and the original data analysis, description of necessary de-identification procedures, and (when required) a copy of the privacy certificate and informed consent protocols.

The plan should be one or two pages in length and include the level of effort associated with meeting archiving requirements.

Note that required data sets are to be submitted 90 days before the end of the project period.

4. **Budget Detail Worksheet and Budget Narrative**

   a. **Budget Detail Worksheet**
      A sample Budget Detail Worksheet can be found at www.ojp.gov/funding/Apply/Resources/BudgetDetailWorksheet.pdf. Applicants that submit their budget in a different format should include the budget categories listed in the sample budget worksheet. (Work associated with satisfying data archiving requirements should be reflected.) BJS expects applicants to provide a thorough narrative to each section of the Budget Detail Worksheet.

      For questions pertaining to budget and examples of allowable and unallowable costs, see the Financial Guide at www.ojp.gov/financialguide/index.htm.

   b. **Budget Narrative**
      The budget narrative should thoroughly and clearly describe <u>every</u> category of expense listed in the Budget Detail Worksheet. OJP expects proposed budgets to be complete, cost effective, and allowable (e.g., reasonable, allocable, and necessary for project activities).

      Applicants should demonstrate in their budget narratives how they will maximize cost effectiveness of grant expenditures. Budget narratives should generally describe cost effectiveness in relation to potential alternatives and the goals of the project. For example, a budget narrative should detail why planned in-person meetings are necessary, or how technology and collaboration with outside organizations could be used to reduce costs, without compromising quality.

      The narrative should be sound mathematically, and correspond with the information and figures provided in the Budget Detail Worksheet. The narrative should explain how the applicant estimated and calculated <u>all</u> costs, and how they are relevant to the completion of the proposed project. The narrative may include tables for clarification purposes but need not be in a spreadsheet format. As with the Budget Detail Worksheet, the Budget Narrative should be broken down by year.

      IMPORTANT NOTE: BJS requires that the application include a separate Budget Detail Worksheet and Budget Narrative for each proposed subcontractor or subrecipient of funds associated with the proposed program.

   c. **Non-Competitive Procurement Contracts In Excess of Simplified Acquisition Threshold**
      If an applicant proposes to make one or more non-competitive procurements of products or services, where the non-competitive procurement will exceed the simplified

acquisition threshold (also known as the small purchase threshold), which is currently set at $150,000, the application should address the considerations outlined in the Financial Guide.

d. Pre-Agreement Cost Approvals

For information on pre-agreement costs approvals, see Section B. Federal Award Information.

5. Indirect Cost Rate Agreement (if applicable)

Indirect costs are allowed only if the applicant has a current federally approved indirect cost rate. (This requirement does not apply to units of local government.) Attach a copy of the federally approved indirect cost rate agreement to the application. Applicants that do not have an approved rate may request one through their cognizant federal agency, which will review all documentation and approve a rate for the applicant organization, or, if the applicant's accounting system permits, costs may be allocated in the direct cost categories. For the definition of Cognizant Federal Agency, see the "Glossary of Terms" in the Financial Guide. For assistance with identifying your cognizant agency, please contact the Customer Service Center at 800-458-0786 or at ask.ocfo@usdoj.gov. If DOJ is the cognizant federal agency, applicants may obtain information needed to submit an indirect cost rate proposal at www.ojp.gov/funding/Apply/Resources/IndirectCosts.pdf.

6. Tribal Authorizing Resolution (if applicable)

Tribes, tribal organizations, or third parties proposing to provide direct services or assistance to residents on tribal lands should include in their applications a resolution, a letter, affidavit, or other documentation, as appropriate, that certifies that the applicant has the legal authority from the tribe(s) to implement the proposed project on tribal lands. In those instances when an organization or consortium of tribes applies for a grant on behalf of a tribe or multiple specific tribes, the application should include appropriate legal documentation, as described above, from all tribes that would receive services or assistance under the grant. A consortium of tribes for which existing consortium bylaws allow action without support from all tribes in the consortium (i.e., without an authorizing resolution or comparable legal documentation from each tribal governing body) may submit, instead, a copy of its consortium bylaws with the application.

Applicants unable to submit an application that includes a fully executed (i.e., signed) copy of appropriate legal documentation, as described above, consistent with the applicable tribe's governance structure, should submit, at a minimum, an unsigned, draft version of such legal documentation as part of its application (except for cases in which, with respect to a tribal consortium applicant, consortium bylaws allow action without the support of all consortium member tribes). If selected for funding, BJS will make use of and access to funds contingent on receipt of the fully executed legal documentation.

7. Applicant Disclosure of High Risk Status

Applicants are to disclose whether they are currently designated high risk by another federal grant making agency. This includes any status requiring additional oversight by the federal agency due to past programmatic or financial concerns. If an applicant is designated high risk by another federal grant making agency, you must email the following information to OJPComplianceReporting@usdoj.gov at the time of application submission:

- The federal agency that currently designated the applicant as high risk

- Date the applicant was designated high risk
- The high risk point of contact name, phone number, and email address, from that federal agency
- Reasons for the high risk status.

OJP seeks this information to ensure appropriate federal oversight of any grant award. Unlike the Excluded Parties List, this high risk information does not disqualify any organization from receiving an OJP award. However, additional grant oversight may be included, if necessary, in award documentation.

8. Additional Attachments

a. Applicant disclosure of pending applications[5]

Applicants are to disclose whether they have pending applications for federally funded grants or subgrants (including cooperative agreements) that include requests for funding to support the same project being proposed under this solicitation and will cover the identical cost items outlined in the budget narrative and worksheet in the application under this solicitation. The disclosure should include both direct applications for federal funding (e.g., applications to federal agencies) and indirect applications for such funding (e.g., applications to state agencies that will subaward federal funds).

OJP seeks this information to help avoid any inappropriate duplication of funding. Leveraging multiple funding sources in a complementary manner to implement comprehensive programs or projects is encouraged and is not seen as inappropriate duplication.

Applicants that have pending applications as described above are to provide the following information about pending applications submitted within the last 12 months:

- The federal or state funding agency
- The solicitation name/project name
- The point of contact information at the applicable funding agency.

Federal or State Funding Agency	Solicitation Name/Project Name	Name/Phone/E-mail for Point of Contact at Funding Agency
DOJ/COPS	COPS Hiring Program	Jane Doe, 202/000-0000; jane.doe@usdoj.gov
HHS/ Substance Abuse & Mental Health Services Administration	Drug Free Communities Mentoring Program/ North County Youth Mentoring Program	John Doe, 202/000-0000; john.doe@hhs.gov

---

[5] Typically, the applicant is not the principal investigator; rather, the applicant, most frequently, is the institution, organization, or company in which the principal investigator is employed.

Applicants should include the table as a separate attachment, with the file name "Disclosure of Pending Applications," to their application. Applicants that do not have pending applications as described above are to include a statement to this effect in the separate attachment page (e.g., "[Applicant Name on SF-424] does not have pending applications submitted within the last 12 months for federally funded grants or subgrants (including cooperative agreements) that include requests for funding to support the same project being proposed under this solicitation and will cover the identical cost items outlined in the budget narrative and worksheet in the application under this solicitation.").

b. **Research and Evaluation Independence and Integrity**

If a proposal involves research and/or evaluation, regardless of the proposal's other merits, in order to receive funds, the applicant must demonstrate research/evaluation independence, including appropriate safeguards to ensure research/evaluation objectivity and integrity, both in this proposal and as it may relate to the applicant's other current or prior related projects. This documentation may be included as an attachment to the application which addresses BOTH i. and ii. below.

i. For purposes of this solicitation, applicants must document research and evaluation independence and integrity by including, at a minimum, one of the following two items:

    a. A specific assurance that the applicant has reviewed its proposal to identify any research integrity issues (including all principal investigators and subrecipients) and it has concluded that the design, conduct, or reporting of data collection, research, and evaluation funded by BJS grants, cooperative agreements, or contracts will not be biased by any personal or financial conflict of interest on the part of its staff, consultants, and/or subrecipients responsible for the research and evaluation or on the part of the applicant organization.

OR

    b. A specific listing of actual or perceived conflicts of interest that the applicant has identified in relation to this proposal. These conflicts could be either personal (related to specific staff, consultants, and/or subrecipients) or organizational (related to the applicant or any subgrantee organization). Examples of potential investigator (or other personal) conflict situations may include, but are not limited to, those in which an investigator would be in a position to evaluate a spouse's work product (actual conflict), or an investigator would be in a position to evaluate the work of a former or current colleague (potential apparent conflict). With regard to potential organizational conflicts of interest, as one example, generally an organization could not be given a grant to evaluate a project if that organization had itself provided substantial prior technical assistance to that specific project or a location implementing the project (whether funded by OJP or other sources), as the organization in such an instance would appear to be evaluating the effectiveness of its own prior work. The key is whether a reasonable person understanding all of the facts would be able to have confidence that the results of any research or evaluation project are objective and reliable. Any outside personal or financial interest that casts doubt on that objectivity and reliability of an evaluation or research product is a problem and must be disclosed.

ii. In addition, for purposes of this solicitation applicants must address the issue of possible mitigation of research integrity concerns by including, at a minimum, one of the following two items:

a. If an applicant reasonably believes that no potential personal or organizational conflicts of interest exist, then the applicant should provide a brief narrative explanation of how and why it reached that conclusion. Applicants MUST also include an explanation of the specific processes and procedures that the applicant will put in place to identify and eliminate (or, at the very least, mitigate) potential personal or financial conflicts of interest on the part of its staff, consultants, and/or subrecipients for this particular project, should that be necessary during the grant period. Documentation that may be helpful in this regard could include organizational codes of ethics/conduct or policies regarding organizational, personal, and financial conflicts of interest.

OR

b. If the applicant has identified specific personal or organizational conflicts of interest in its proposal during this review, the applicant must propose a specific and robust mitigation plan to address conflicts noted above. At a minimum, the plan must include specific processes and procedures that the applicant will put in place to eliminate (or, at the very least, mitigate) potential personal or financial conflicts of interest on the part of its staff, consultants, and/or subrecipients for this particular project, should that be necessary during the grant period. Documentation that may be helpful in this regard could include organizational codes of ethics/conduct or policies regarding organizational, personal, and financial conflicts of interest. There is no guarantee that the plan, if any, will be accepted as proposed.

Considerations in assessing research and evaluation independence and integrity will include, but are not be limited to, the adequacy of the applicant's efforts to identify factors that could affect the objectivity or integrity of the proposed staff and/or the organization in carrying out the research, development, or evaluation activity; and the adequacy of the applicant's existing or proposed remedies to control any such factors.

9. **Financial Management and System of Internal Controls Questionnaire**
In accordance with 2 CFR 200.205, federal agencies must have in place a framework for evaluating the risks posed by applicants before they receive a federal award. To facilitate part of this risk evaluation, **all** applicants (other than an individual) are to download, complete, and submit this form.

10. **Disclosure of Lobbying Activities**
All applicants must complete this information. Applicants that expend any funds for lobbying activities are to provide the detailed information requested on the form Disclosure of Lobbying Activities (SF-LLL). Applicants that do not expend any funds for lobbying activities

are to enter "N/A" in the text boxes for item 10 ("a. Name and Address of Lobbying Registrant" and "b. Individuals Performing Services").

How to Apply
Applicants must register in, and submit applications through Grants.gov, a "one-stop storefront" to find federal funding opportunities and apply for funding. Find complete instructions on how to register and submit an application at www.Grants.gov. Applicants that experience technical difficulties during this process should call the Grants.gov Customer Support Hotline at **800-518-4726** or **606-545-5035**, 24 hours a day, 7 days a week, except federal holidays. Registering with Grants.gov is a one-time process; however, **processing delays may occur, and it can take several weeks** for first-time registrants to receive confirmation and a user password. OJP encourages applicants to **register several weeks before** the application submission deadline. In addition, OJP urges applicants to submit applications 72 hours prior to the application due date to allow time to receive validation messages or rejection notifications from Grants.gov, and to correct in a timely fashion any problems that may have caused a rejection notification.

BJS strongly encourages all prospective applicants to sign up for Grants.gov email notifications regarding this solicitation. If this solicitation is cancelled or modified, individuals who sign up with Grants.gov for updates will be automatically notified.

Note on File Names and File Types: Grants.gov only permits the use of certain specific characters in names of attachment files. Valid file names may include only the characters shown in the table below. Grants.gov is designed to reject any application that includes an attachment(s) with a file name that contains any characters not shown in the table below. Grants.gov is designed to forward successfully submitted applications to OJP's Grants Management System (GMS).

Characters	Special Characters		
Upper case (A – Z)	Parenthesis ( )	Curly braces { }	Square brackets [ ]
Lower case (a – z)	Ampersand (&)	Tilde (~)	Exclamation point (!)
Underscore (__)	Comma (,)	Semicolon (;)	Apostrophe (')
Hyphen (-)	At sign (@)	Number sign (#)	Dollar sign ($)
Space	Percent sign (%)	Plus sign (+)	Equal sign (=)
Period (.)	**When using the ampersand (&) in XML, applicants must use the "&" format.**		

GMS does not accept executable file types as application attachments. These disallowed file types include, but are not limited to, the following extensions: ".com," ".bat," ".exe," ".vbs," ".cfg," ".dat," ".db," ".dbf," ".dll," ".ini," ".log," ".ora," ".sys," and ".zip." GMS may reject applications with files that use these extensions. It is important to allow time to change the type of file(s) if the application is rejected.

All applicants are required to complete the following steps:

OJP may not make a federal award to an applicant until the applicant has complied with all applicable DUNS and SAM requirements. If an applicant has not fully complied with the requirements by the time the federal awarding agency is ready to make a federal award, the federal awarding agency may determine that the applicant is not qualified to receive a federal award and use that determination as a basis for making a federal award to another applicant.

1. **Acquire a Data Universal Numbering System (DUNS) number.** In general, the Office of Management and Budget requires that all applicants (other than individuals) for federal funds include a DUNS number in their applications for a new award or a supplement to an existing award. A DUNS number is a unique nine-digit sequence recognized as the universal standard for identifying and differentiating entities receiving federal funds. The identifier is used for tracking purposes and to validate address and point of contact information for federal assistance applicants, recipients, and subrecipients. The DUNS number will be used throughout the grant life cycle. Obtaining a DUNS number is a free, one-time activity. Call Dun and Bradstreet at 866-705-5711 to obtain a DUNS number or apply online at www.dnb.com. A DUNS number is usually received within 1–2 business days.

2. **Acquire registration with the System for Award Management (SAM).** SAM is the repository for standard information about federal financial assistance applicants, recipients, and subrecipients. OJP requires all applicants (other than individuals) for federal financial assistance to maintain current registrations in the SAM database. Applicants must be registered in SAM to successfully register in Grants.gov. Applicants must **update or renew their SAM registration annually** to maintain an active status.

   Applications cannot be successfully submitted in Grants.gov until Grants.gov receives the SAM registration information. The information transfer from SAM to Grants.gov can take up to 48 hours. OJP recommends that the applicant register or renew registration with SAM as early as possible.

   Information about SAM registration procedures can be accessed at www.sam.gov.

3. **Acquire an Authorized Organization Representative (AOR) and a Grants.gov username and password**. Complete the AOR profile on Grants.gov and create a username and password. The applicant organization's DUNS number must be used to complete this step. For more information about the registration process, go to www.grants.gov/web/grants/register.html.

4. **Acquire confirmation for the AOR from the E-Business Point of Contact (E-Biz POC).** The E-Biz POC at the applicant organization must log into Grants.gov to confirm the applicant organization's AOR. Note that an organization can have more than one AOR.

5. **Search for the funding opportunity on Grants.gov.** Use the following identifying information when searching for the funding opportunity on Grants.gov. The Catalog of Federal Domestic Assistance number for this solicitation is 16.734, titled "Special Data Collections and Statistical Studies" and the funding opportunity number is BJS-2015-4166.

6. **Submit a valid application consistent with this solicitation by following the directions in Grants.gov.** Within 24–48 hours after submitting the electronic application, the applicant should receive two notifications from Grants.gov. The first will confirm the receipt of the application and the second will state whether the application has been successfully validated, or rejected due to errors, with an explanation. It is possible to first receive a message indicating that the application is received and then receive a rejection notice a few minutes or hours later. Submitting well ahead of the deadline provides time to correct the problem(s) that caused the rejection. **Important:** OJP urges applicants to submit applications **at least 72 hours prior** to the application due date to allow time to receive

validation messages or rejection notifications from Grants.gov, and to correct in a timely fashion any problems that may have caused a rejection notification.

Click here for further details on DUNS, SAM, and Grants.gov registration steps and timeframes.

Note: Duplicate Applications
If an applicant submits multiple versions of the same application, BJS will review <u>only</u> the most recent system-validated version submitted. See Note on File Names and File Types under How To Apply.

Experiencing Unforeseen Grants.gov Technical Issues
Applicants that experience unforeseen Grants.gov technical issues beyond their control that prevent them from submitting their application by the deadline must contact the Grants.gov Customer Support Hotline or the SAM Help Desk to report the technical issue and receive a tracking number. Then applicant must email the BJS contact identified in the Contact Information section on page 2 **within 24 hours after the application deadline** and request approval to submit their application. The email must describe the technical difficulties, and include a timeline of the applicant's submission efforts, the complete grant application, the applicant's DUNS number, and any Grants.gov Help Desk or SAM tracking number(s). **Note: BJS does not automatically approve requests.** After the program office reviews the submission, and contacts the Grants.gov or SAM Help Desks to validate the reported technical issues, OJP will inform the applicant whether the request to submit a late application has been approved or denied. If OJP determines that the applicant failed to follow all required procedures, which resulted in an untimely application submission, OJP will deny the applicant's request to submit their application.

The following conditions are generally insufficient to justify late submissions:

- Failure to register in SAM or Grants.gov in sufficient time
- Failure to follow Grants.gov instructions on how to register and apply as posted on its website
- Failure to follow each instruction in the OJP solicitation
- Technical issues with the applicant's computer or information technology environment, including firewalls.

Notifications regarding known technical problems with Grants.gov, if any, are posted at the top of the OJP funding web page at www.ojp.gov/funding/Explore/CurrentFundingOpportunities.htm.

E. Application Review Information

Selection Criteria
Applications that meet basic minimum requirements will be evaluated by peer reviewers using the following review criteria.

Statement of the Problem (10%)—Applicants must demonstrate a clear understanding of the project and the SJIC program goals of (a) improving the timeliness of the SJIC data, (b) enhancing the reliability of the data, (c) fostering strong working relationships with and among data providers, (d) improving responsiveness to stakeholder needs, and (e) developing and implementing efficient data collection mechanisms.

Applications must demonstrate—

1. Understanding of the SJIC goals.
2. Knowledge of issues facing Indian country jails, the need to provide jails in Indian country agencies with the information they need, and the challenges faced by Indian country agencies in gathering and reporting data.
3. Knowledge of methods for improving timely survey response.
4. Understanding of the value of the SJIC project to the corrections' field.

Project Design and Implementation (Goals and Objectives) (25%)—Applicants must demonstrate that they can design and implement a high-quality project. Applications should demonstrate—

1. A plan for efficiently and cost-effectively administering establishment surveys to Indian country agencies that collect and process establishment data.
2. An understanding of the challenges facing Indian country jail respondents in providing data to meet BJS standards and an approach that recognizes and addresses these challenges.
3. The capacity to produce statistical tables and conduct statistical analysis in a timely manner that meets BJS data quality standards and BJS production timelines.
4. Sound proposed procedures for carrying out the project tasks and meeting the project deliverable time frames, including a commitment to identifying and communicating potential problems to be addressed before they become an issue, and a plan for up-to-date tracking and reporting of data collection progress.

Capabilities and Competencies (35%)—Applicants must demonstrate that they have the appropriate corporate and staff capabilities and experience to conduct the work outlined in the project tasks. These requirements include—

1. Qualifications, demonstrated ability, and experience of the proposed staff who will manage the project and those who will have day-to-day data collection responsibilities in the use of accepted survey research methods in the following areas: (a) questionnaire design; (b) collection of administrative data from hard to reach agencies; (c) cleaning and verifying data, and providing files that exhibit a high degree of accuracy; (d) adjusting for nonresponse, including multiple methods of imputation; (e) conducting independent analysis of data; and (f) the production of public use datasets and documentation that require a high degree of attention to detail.
2. Qualifications, demonstrated ability, and experience of the information technology staff, and the capacity of the computing environment, for developing electronic based data collection tools (pending results of feasibility study), preparation of datasets for statistical analysis, and preparing statistical reports.
3. An adequate management plan for the project, including sufficient delineation of project tasks to provide a full understanding of how project resources will be used.
4. Adequate management oversight and quality control procedures.
5. Successful past performance of the proposed project team in addressing the key objectives for the project.
6. Tribal affiliation/participation.
7. Demonstrated knowledge of the extant literature on Native American and indigenous research and evaluation to include strength of citations and other appropriate information to support the understanding of the problem.

8. Demonstrated knowledge of the U.S. and tribal criminal justice systems and jurisdictional issues.
9. Demonstrated knowledge of potential limitations and challenges of conducting surveys, research in Indian Country and in Alaska Native villages with members of indigenous communities on sensitive topics.
10. Demonstrated knowledge of and expertise with tribal communities.
11. Demonstrated understanding of the complexity of the problems faced by Native Americans living in tribal communities.
12. Clarity of the problem statement and its importance to the field of study.
13. Demonstrated connection between problem and proposed survey.
14. Effort to ensure survey methods are respectful of tribal sovereignty, customs, and traditions.

Budget (15%)—Applicants must demonstrate awareness of methods for using budgetary resources efficiently and effectively and demonstrate appropriate internal controls over these resources.
1. The appropriateness of the proposed budget for the level of effort outlined in the project plans.
2. Adequate and efficient assignment of staff to tasks.
3. Adequate budgetary controls to ensure that resources are managed effectively and in compliance with federal regulations.

Peer reviewers will consider and may comment on the following additional items in the context of scientific and technical merit.
1. Total cost of the project relative to the perceived benefit (cost effectiveness)
2. Appropriateness of the budget relative to the level of effort
3. Use of existing resources to conserve costs
4. Proposed budget alignment with proposed project activities

Impact/Outcomes and Evaluation (15%)—Evaluation is critical for ensuring that each BJS project is operating as designed and achieving its goals and objectives. Applicants must—
1. Provide a plan for assessing the effectiveness of the SJIC project in meeting project goals and objectives and in documenting project accomplishments, and
2. Describe how they will assess performance in attaining the project outcomes.

Goals and objectives must be clearly stated, and links between project activities and objectives and performance measures must be identified. Performance measures will address a mix of immediate and intermediate outcomes, and as appropriate and feasible, information on long-term impact of the project on Indian country and the corrections field.

Plan for Dissemination to Broader Audiences (if applicable to the proposed project)

Peer reviewers may comment—in the context of scientific and technical merit—on the proposed plan (if any) to produce or to make available to broader interested audiences, such as criminal/juvenile justice practitioners or policymakers, summary information from the planned scholarly products of the project.

Review Process

OJP is committed to ensuring a fair and open process for awarding grants. BJS reviews the application to make sure that the information presented is reasonable, understandable, measurable, and achievable, as well as consistent with the solicitation.

Peer reviewers will review the applications submitted under this solicitation that meet basic minimum requirements. For purposes of assessing whether applicants have met basic minimum requirements, OJP screens applications for compliance with specified program requirements to help determine which applications should proceed to further consideration for award. Although program requirements may vary, the following are common requirements applicable to all solicitations for funding under OJP grant programs:

- Applications must be submitted by an eligible type of applicant
- Applications must request funding within programmatic funding constraints (if applicable)
- Applications must be responsive to the scope of the solicitation
- Applications must include all items designated as "critical elements"
- Applicants will be checked against the General Services Administration's Excluded Parties List.

For a list of critical elements, see "What an Application Should Include" under Section D. Application and Submission Information.

BJS may use internal peer reviewers, external peer reviewers, or a combination, to assess applications meeting basic minimum requirements on technical merit using the solicitation's selection criteria. An external peer reviewer is an expert in the subject matter of a given solicitation who is not a current DOJ employee. An internal reviewer is a current DOJ employee who is well-versed or has expertise in the subject matter of this solicitation. A peer review panel will evaluate, score, and rate applications that meet basic minimum requirements.

Reviewers will complete the OPM online training program "Working Effectively With Tribal Governments" with the completion certificate being submitted prior to being selected as reviewer.

OJP reviews applications for potential discretionary awards to evaluate the risks posed by applicants before they receive an award. This review may include but is not limited to the following:

1. Financial stability and fiscal integrity
2. Quality of management systems and ability to meet the management standards prescribed in the Financial Guide
3. History of performance
4. Reports and findings from audits
5. The applicant's ability to effectively implement statutory, regulatory, or other requirements imposed on non-federal entities
6. Proposed costs to determine if the Budget Detail Worksheet and Budget Narrative accurately explain project costs, and whether those costs are reasonable, necessary, and allowable under applicable federal cost principles and agency regulations.

All final award decisions will be made by the director of the Bureau of Justice Statistics. Peer reviewers' ratings and any resulting recommendations are advisory only, although their views are considered carefully. In addition to peer review ratings, considerations for award recommendations and decisions may include, but are not limited to, planned scholarly products, proposed budgets, past performance (including scholarly products) under prior BJS and OJP awards, research independence and integrity, strategic priorities, and available funding when making awards.

F. Federal Award Administration Information

Federal Award Notices

OJP award notification will be sent from GMS. Recipients will be required to login; accept any outstanding assurances and certifications on the award; designate a financial point of contact; and review, sign, and accept the award. The award acceptance process involves physical signature of the award document by the authorized representative and the scanning of the fully-executed award document to OJP.

Administrative, National Policy, and other Legal Requirements

If selected for funding, in addition to implementing the funded project consistent with the agency-approved project proposal and budget, the recipient must comply with award terms and conditions, and other legal requirements, that are included in the award, incorporated into the award by reference, or are otherwise applicable to the award. OJP strongly encourages prospective applicants to review the information pertaining to these requirements **prior** to submitting an application. To assist applicants and recipients in accessing and reviewing this information, OJP has placed it on its Solicitation Requirements page of the OJP Funding Resource Center.

Please note in particular the following two forms, which applicants must submit in GMS prior to the receipt of any award funds, as each details legal requirements with which applicants must provide specific assurances and certifications of compliance. Applicants may view these forms in the OJP Funding Resource Center and are strongly encouraged to review and consider them carefully prior to making an application for OJP grant funds.

- Certifications Regarding Lobbying; Debarment, Suspension and Other Responsibility Matters; and Drug-Free Workplace Requirements

- Standard Assurances

Upon grant approval, OJP electronically transmits (via GMS) the award document to the prospective award recipient. In addition to other award information, the award document contains award terms and conditions that specify national policy requirements[6] with which recipients of federal funding must comply; uniform administrative requirements, cost principles, and audit requirements; and program-specific terms and conditions required based on applicable program (statutory) authority or requirements set forth in OJP solicitations and program announcements. For example, certain efforts may call for special requirements, terms, or conditions relating to intellectual property, data/information-sharing or -access, or information

---

[6] See generally 2 CFR 200.300 (provides a general description of national policy requirements typically applicable to recipients of federal awards, including the Federal Funding Accountability and Transparency Act of 2006 (FFATA)).

security; or audit requirements, expenditures and milestones, or publications and/or press releases.

OJP also may place additional terms and conditions on an award based on its risk assessment of the applicant, or for other reasons it determines necessary to fulfill the goals and objectives of the program.

Prospective applicants may access and review the text of mandatory conditions OJP includes in all OJP awards, as well as the text of certain other conditions, such as administrative conditions, via OJP's Mandatory Award Terms and Conditions page of the Funding Resource Center.

As stated above, BJS expects that it will make any award from this solicitation in the form of a cooperative agreement. Cooperative agreement awards include standard "federal involvement" conditions that describe the general allocation of responsibility for execution of the funded program. Generally stated, under cooperative agreement awards, responsibility for the day-to-day conduct of the funded project rests with the recipient in implementing the funded and approved proposal and budget, and the award terms and conditions. Responsibility for oversight and redirection of the project, if necessary, rests with BJS.

In addition to any "federal involvement" condition(s), OJP cooperative agreement awards include a special condition specifying certain reporting requirements required in connection with conferences, meetings, retreats, seminars, symposium, training activities, or similar events funded under the award, consistent with OJP policy and guidance on "conference" approval, planning, and reporting.

BJS awards made under this kind of solicitation will also typically include a number of special conditions including, among others, the following four:

- First, the project will be funded as a cooperative agreement. The basis for using a cooperative agreement is the substantial involvement of BJS in providing information, guidance, and direction regarding special data collections and the development of statistical studies. BJS will exercise general approval over the entire project subject to the recipient's rights to disclose and publish certain information after review and comment by BJS, as set forth in this solicitation.

- Second, the award recipient will agree that no funds provided may be used to author or prepare reports, journal articles, speeches or studies, or other publications without the prior written approval of BJS, regardless of whether the data used in the publications or other releases are publicly available.

- Third, BJS will retain all rights to exclusive use of the data until BJS releases the public-use dataset, which will be available to the public via the Internet and at the National Criminal Justice Data Archives at the University of Michigan. The award recipient will not be able to release or disclose any data collected through this cooperative agreement without prior written BJS approval or until the dataset has been released to the public. This includes, but is not limited to, presentations at professional conferences and meetings, press releases, and grant applications. Protected data includes all data collected by BJS, or on behalf of, BJS that BJS has not yet released to the public, but does not include aggregate results derived from the data by the recipient provided that such results do not contain any confidential, proprietary, or personally identifiable information.

- Fourth, the award recipient will retain a nonexclusive use of any methodological findings derived by the recipient or BJS from the project, subject to the following condition: Only with the prior review and written comment by BJS, which includes the mutual agreement on the representation of BJS methodologies, may the recipient publicly disclose its or BJS's methodologies derived from the project prior to the release of the dataset. Such review and comment period shall not exceed forty-five (45) days of receipt of the proposed publication. Any such disclosures of the recipient's or BJS's methodologies must be public in nature and contribute meaningfully to the development and advancement of social science research. Public disclosure may include, but is not limited to, presentations at professional conferences and meetings, articles appearing in widely distributed publications, and Internet postings or similar outlets that constitute a broad public release of the methodological information.

General Information About Post-Federal Award Reporting Requirements
Recipients must submit quarterly financial reports, select semi-annual progress reports, final financial and progress reports, and, if applicable, an annual audit report in accordance with 2 CFR Part 200. Applicants should anticipate that progress reports will be required to follow the non-budgetary components of the Research Performance Progress Report (RPPR) template/format. General information on RPPRs may be found at www.nsf.gov/bfa/dias/policy/rppr/. Future awards and fund drawdowns may be withheld if reports are delinquent.

Special reporting requirements may be required by OJP depending on the statutory, legislative or administrative requirements of the recipient or the program.

As indicated earlier in this solicitation, BJS recognizes that scholarly products may result from an award under this solicitation. Applicants should review the Goals, Objectives, Deliverables, and Expected Scholarly Products segment of the "Program-Specific Information" section of this solicitation, as well as the "Performance Measures" section. In addition to any specific expectation of scholarly products, successful applicants under this solicitation will be required to submit the following deliverables regarding the work funded by the BJS award.

Draft and Final Summary Overview of the Work Conducted under the Award
The overview is expected to provide an overall summary of the work under, and results of, the project funded by BJS under this solicitation. Among other things, the summary overview should address the purpose of the project, project subjects (if applicable), project design and methods, data analysis, project findings, and implications for criminal justice policy and practice in the United States.

A draft summary overview no longer than 10 pages long (double-spaced) is to be submitted 90 days prior to the end of the project period for BJS review and comment.

Required Data Sets and Associated Files and Documentation
As discussed earlier, BJS requires recipients of an award under this solicitation to submit to NACJD all datasets that result in whole or in part from the work funded by BJS, along with the final Data Management Plan, associated files, and any documentation necessary to allow for future efforts by others to reproduce the project's findings and to extend the scientific value of the data set through secondary analysis. All datasets and necessary documentation are to be

submitted 90 days prior to the end of the project period. For more information, see the "Program Narrative" section of <u>What an Application Should Include</u>.

G. Federal Awarding Agency Contact(s)

For additional Federal Awarding Agency Contact(s), see the Title page.

For additional contact information for Grants.gov, see the Title page.

H. Other Information

Provide Feedback to OJP

To assist OJP in improving its application and award processes, we encourage applicants to provide feedback on this solicitation, the application submission process, and the application review/peer review process. Provide feedback to <u>OJPSolicitationFeedback@usdoj.gov</u>.

IMPORTANT: This email is for feedback and suggestions only. Replies are not sent from this mailbox. If you have specific questions on any program or technical aspect of the solicitation, you must directly contact the appropriate number or email listed on the front of this solicitation document. These contacts are provided to help ensure that you can directly reach an individual who can address your specific questions in a timely manner.

If you are interested in being a reviewer for other OJP grant applications, please email your resume to <u>ojppeerreview@lmbps.com</u>. The OJP Solicitation Feedback email account will not forward your resume. Note: Neither you nor anyone else from your organization can be a peer reviewer in a competition in which you or your organization have submitted an application.

Application Checklist

Annual Survey of Jails in Indian Country, 2016–2019

This application checklist has been created to assist in developing an application.

What an Applicant Should Do:

Prior to Registering in Grants.gov:
_____ Acquire a DUNS Number   (see page 27)
_____ Acquire or renew registration with SAM   (see page 27)
To Register with Grants.gov:
_____ Acquire AOR and Grants.gov username/password (see page 27)
_____ Acquire AOR confirmation from the E-Biz POC   (see page 27)
To Find Funding Opportunity:
_____ Search for the funding opportunity on Grants.gov   (see page 27)
_____ Download Funding Opportunity and Application Package   (see page 27)
_____ Sign up for Grants.gov email notifications (optional) (see page 27)
_____ Read **Important Notice: Applying for Grants in Grants.gov**
After application submission, receive Grants.gov email notifications that:
_____ (1) application has been received
_____ (2) application has either been successfully validated or rejected with errors
                                        (see page 27)
If no Grants.gov receipt, and validation or error notifications are received:
_____ contact BJS regarding experiencing technical difficulties
                                        (see page 28)

General Requirements:

_____ Review the Solicitation Requirements in the OJP Funding Resource Center.

What an Application Should Include:

_____ Application for Federal Assistance (SF-424)   (see page 14)
_____ Project Abstract   (see page 14)
_____ Program Narrative   (see page 15)
_____ Appendices   (see page 19)
_____ Budget Detail Worksheet   (see page 21)
_____ Budget Narrative   (see page 21)
        _____ Employee Compensation Waiver request and justification (if applicable)   (see page 12)
        _____ Read OJP policy and guidance on "conference" approval, planning, and reporting available at www.ojp.gov/funding/confcost.htm
                                        (see page 13)
_____ Disclosure of Lobbying Activities (SF-LLL)   (see page 25)
_____ Indirect Cost Rate Agreement (if applicable)   (see page 22)
_____ Tribal Authorizing Resolution (if applicable)   (see page 22)
_____ Applicant Disclosure of High Risk Status   (see page 22)

_____ Additional Attachments
    _____ Privacy Certification   (see page 20)
    _____ Human Subjects Protection Certification of Compliance (see page 20)
        _____ Applicant Disclosure of Pending Applications (see page 23)
        _____ Research and Evaluation Independence and Integrity
                                      (see page 24)
 _____ Financial Management and System of Internal Controls Questionnaire (if applicable)
                                          (see page 25)